Reflections

On My Eternal Light

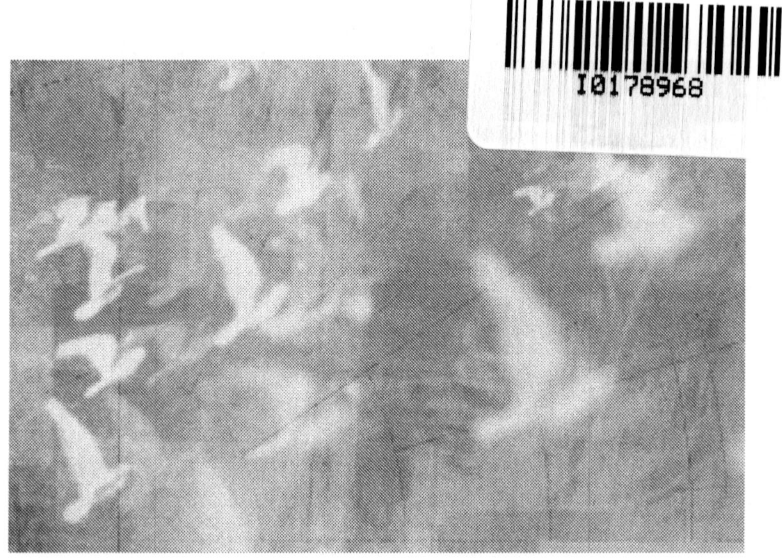

Spiritual Messages from the Masters

channeled by
Jan Manzi

Reflections

On My Eternal Light Spiritual Messages from the Masters

ISBN 0-9678721-3-8

Published by:

Infinite Light Healing Studies Center, Inc.
Publishing Division
P.O. Box 130, Hartsel, CO 80449

www.infinitelight.com

Cover Design by: Laurelle Shanti Gaia

Infinite Light Publishing

Our Mission . . .

... is to publish spiritually inspired books, meditation CDs, and self study programs. We also provide training programs, healing tools and educational materials, which promote the development of wellness consciousness, peace and earth healing.

In addition, we offer distant energy healing sessions, at no cost, through a worldwide network of light workers and peace weavers. If you would like to be of service through this network, please contact us through our publishing website www.infinitelight.com

May Peace Prevail On Earth
Om Shanti Gaia

❧ ✻ ☙

Foreword

by Laurelle Shanti Gaia

I am in constant amazement at the power of God to bring people together to facilitate the spiritual unfoldment of humanity. This very same limitless power is responsible for the publishing of this beautiful book, at this time. A very special thank you goes out to Jan Manzi, Jill Wood, Burton Johnson, and the 44 sisters.

It is an honor to play a part in bringing "Reflections on My Eternal Light" to you.

There is great wisdom in the words contained within this treasury of Divine blessings. Jan Manzi has brought them forth with a pure heart, and clear intention to be of service. She is a true instrument through which the Masters share their song of love with us.

This work of spiritual artistry is a great gift to humanity. It was offered to us by magnificent celestial beings of light who have come forth to help humanity awaken to the age of peace.

Whether you read this book from cover to cover, or, you hold it in your hands while you pray for guidance . . . "Reflections" will absolutely speak to the very heart of your soul.

In the Light of the Creator . . .

We See Only Love and We Are Only Peace

Introduction

In the year of 1993, I was guided to move to Arizona from Connecticut where I had resided for most of my life. I did not understand why, for my plans had been to retire to Florida, however there was a sense within me that this was necessary, and was where I belonged. I thought this move was because of my need to be away from the cold, damp winters of Connecticut. My family and some of my friends thought I was not quite in my right mind, I wondered also.

In Payson, Arizona, a woman named Bernetta who was a Flower Essence Channel, was introduced to me and consequently channeled information for me from St. Germain. From this and subsequent channels from the Ascended Masters, through Bernetta, I was given information that I was a healer, a channel, a teacher, and that I would write a book and give workshops.

How could this be, for I was so immersed into third dimensional thinking and action, with my children and granddaughters.

Even though I had studied and taught "A Course in Miracles", in Connecticut and Florida, where I often vacationed, and had started teaching here (for the Course is deeply loved by me), I was unable to grasp these ideas and consequently said "no, to everything the Masters suggested!"

There is a poster hanging on my wall, which signifies the relationship between God and mankind, and whenever I passed this poster, I would touch it in a caressing manner, sometimes weeping and kissing this image, with an intense feeling of great love.

One day after my prayers and meditation I heard a voice say, "Get your pen, dear One." So began an almost daily communication from the Masters. These communications were in most cases, small paragraphs, and sometimes one sentence for the day, and this is how they are presented in this manual.

The Masters sent me to Calgary, Canada, to bring the "Course" and later I went back to teach and conduct a workshop. On my first trip to Canada, I visited Lake Louise, etc., and took many pictures. When I came home there was still film in the camera, so I took two pictures of this poster on my wall that is so dear to me. Imagine, my great surprise when the film was developed, and where the image of God is on the poster, there emerged a great, round white light.

I asked Bernetta if she would channel information about this light for me. Sananda (Jesus) told me that I had a desire to see what my soul looked like, and the poster had been imprinted with the reflection of my soul. He also said this image had been given to me as a gift. Consequently, the title of my manual arose, “Reflections on my Eternal Light”.

Dedication and Acknowledgements

This book is dedicated to All That I Am, Ascended Master Teacher Sananda, Mother Mary, Quan Yin, the Lady of mercy and compassion, Saint Germain and L'Morya. It was and continues to be only through their gentle and loving nudging that I have been able to hear their messages and become willing to put down on paper the information.

My deepest gratitude to these Masters, for my life has surely been changed. I am learning about Love in a manner that totally eluded me in prior times. I cannot define Love for you, however, should you catch a glimpse of Love in these pages, it is a blessing.

I offer a special thank you to Jill Wood, who has been a wonderful friend, and consultant to me. Jill and her spiritual gifts were instrumental in helping me connect with the publisher of "Reflections".

I would like to acknowledge my son Sal, who throughout his life was my teacher, attempting to teach me how to accept the Will of God. I was honored to have him as a son. I would also like to thank my daughter Karen, for her consistency in her love and her faith in me. I am most grateful. Last, but not least, I thank my three grandchildren, Colleen Christian, Sarah Lynn, and Rebecca Ann, for Being Who They Are.

My Prayer

Beloved Father, Divinity of all life,
*the **ALL IN ALL**,*

Hear my Soul cry to Thee
from my heart, for a deeper knowledge
and understanding of Our Oneness.

Increase my love and my capacity
to love so that is all I desire.

Assist me that I may see with Your Eyes,
and hear with Your Ears.

May I speak with Your Wisdom
and grant that my Christed Self
may become manifest in its desire
to love You only.

This is asked through Christ, and So It is.

Mary, the Mother of Jesus

Dear One,

We have brought you here so that you may express love for the Oneness of All life, be it small creature or large animals. Be it the water that falls over these boulders at Horton Creek, or the sun that shines through the trees; these granite rocks about you and the wild roses along the pathway, which is strewn with wild wheat, that carries it's seed for the next season. Feel the gentle breeze that caresses your cheeks, and brings a smile upon your face. The tall pines, dear One, and the aspen that seems to say amongst the pine "make room for me". This small waterfall that becomes a roar, if one closes one's eyes.

Release, dear one, everything that has bound you, whether in this life or others, so in releasing, your cells may become neutral, as St. Germain has mentioned to you. Cast your fears upon the water and know Thy Rod and Thy Staff will comfort thee. The Divine Mind of God is your inheritance and your Divinity is One with God.

Allow the warmth of the sun to permeate every pore of your body, and know this power of the sun is yours. The rock that you sit upon is held together by the power of love (God), otherwise it would disintegrate.

I, Mother Mary, desire for you to write these words;

Humanity must change its ways. Let go of your egos, use the violet flame, beloved people. This is a gift (Violet Flame). Ask us to assist you and we will. *You must ask*, for we cannot interfere with your gift of *free will*, which was given to you from the Father, which allows everything.

The great love of the Father permeates every living being, if only mankind would access that Divine Love that is available, peace would prevail throughout this planet. Mankind has abused its rights and privileges as a species, it has denied the love of the Father, and denied the Divinity of each soul upon this beautiful planet.

Know that as I wrap my arms around each one of you so does the Father. If you only knew of the love the Father has for you, every cell in your body would vibrate in total happiness and joy!

We are on a venture, a joint experience, and we are here to assist you. It is our joy and delight! Beloved children of my heart, hear my plea for you to love one another, as my beloved son Jesus, taught two thousand years ago.

Pick up your pen, Child,

Know that the Father, Universal Mind, forever watches over you, and that the Angelic Beings of Light, wish to tell you that you are greatly loved.

The Divine Oneness of the Father, is Universal. It is One Mind, and One Heart. It is a great and profound Unity and Universal Knowledge that is available to all. Learning the art of listening is allowing your thoughts (ego thoughts), to be set aside. Open your eyes for the inner vision, and open your ears for inner hearing, which comes from the Heart of God. Listen and you will hear us.

Dear Child,

The illumination of the soul is forever brilliant, for it is a pure and total light. The little fetus in a woman's body knows how to form itself and what it will be like at birth. It has planned this entry into life, an agreement that was set in the stars for it's wisdom, and for it's attainment of what it needs to learn, it's lessons, so to speak.

The soul that desires an entrance into this world oftentimes comes to teach its mother and father. The children born in this age are greatly enlightened, the veil is not as heavy, as they are very telepathic and remember more. Indeed every birth is a blessed event.

Beloved Daughter,

I, Mary, desire to convey to you the idea of one perfect cell in the Body of the Father, which is What You Are. When you were a Thought in the Mind of the Creator, your perfection was. How could it be otherwise, for God is perfect?

You speak in your classes that God is a giant firecracker that lit Itself, and the brilliant sparks burst forth in creation. You are a spark of that Divine Source, and the powers of God are within you.

Mankind has been endowed with all knowledge and wisdom, however in the gross denseness of the body, mankind has forgotten Its Divinity and Oneness with the Creator. We are all One

Beloved Child,

Behold the Lamb of God, who some day will lay down with the lion in peace and love. So will it be for mankind. When every human soul knows of its holiness and loves and honors itself, there will be no more division amongst people of the planet Earth.

The meek shall indeed inherit the earth, for is not love soft, gentle, kind and always in a state of Beingness?

The eternal bliss of the Father is yours. God has endowed you with all of Himself. Divinity is always within you. Do not look outside of yourself for your answers, for they are within your heart. Go in peace and love this day.

Beloved Child,

Loving in a manner that is satisfying to you and to the loved one, is a delightful experience. The expression of love is God the Creator. Love is the only way; no matter how you love, it is the intent in the soul, the desire. Love has been given many names, love of family, love of companion, love of self, love of children, love of the Creator, all beautiful Light.

My son, Jesus came to teach this message of love, forgiveness and healing.

Child,

I, Mary, wish to tell you to continue praying for mankind. When one prays for mankind, the consciousness is lifted. Prayers are collective and have a rippling effect, they stream forth and not only reach the parameters of the earth, but prayers do go into other realms and universes. Prayers are thought forms, energy. Love energy, which is from our Universal Father, is the most powerful force. There is nothing else for All is Love.

❧ ✻ ☙

Dear One,

Surround Child, in your prayers, the entire planet with its people upon it in the Violet Ray of transmutation. See if you can do this daily.

I go in peace and peace to you. Know that we are with you always and that we love you.

❧ ✻ ☙

ꕥ ✻ ꕥ

Daughter of the Light,

I, Mother Mary, wish to say to you, dear One, that the unity of the heart, mind and soul is held together by the force of the Love of our Creator. This powerful Source allows all things upon this planet for your ***experience***, not for judgement. There is nothing to judge, for you came here to experience. You came to feel your intuitions, and your five senses of taste, smell, touch, seeing and hearing; to experience these sensations, all the while never forgetting the Source of all life, our Creator.

Mankind has become gross sinking into the mire of materialism, dear One, and this has taken away from the idea of God as all Power and Love, and instead the materialism has become yet another idol, as in the days of yore. When will mankind realize its' Godliness, and its' Holiness?

Plant a seed of love and forgiveness, then it is up to the individual whether to use this seed of love and forgiveness. Each person is on their path, some karmic and some not.

Stay in your power, in your love and in the grace of the Father. We support and love you.

ꕥ ✻ ꕥ

Dear One,

You desire this information. The Body of God, one cell, with it's billions of cells, all comprise to make up the wholeness of the Creator. The God Source, Alpha/Omega is incomplete without you. It knows all Its' members and you are the remembrance of the Body of God, a Divine Thought of the Creator.

I leave you in peace, dear One.

Dear One,

At this time of the year, mankind rejoices in celebration at the birth of my beloved Son. It was set in the plan of God, for a Savior, a grand teacher, who would remind mankind of it's Divinity, it's Oneness with God. How blessed was I to be graced with this Gift from the Father! What a joy my son was to my heart, and his message was simple, love and forgiveness, was it not!

At this time great love is poured on this planet, for the purification of souls. I, Mary and my Son are infusing love upon humanity. We will make ourselves known and be seen by multitudes so that humanity may believe that God reigns and they will know there is no death.

Pray for humanity and for the spark of love to be expanded, for this is the God force of each human being.

Dear Daughter of the Light,

I, Mary, tell you that your love reaches us and we are aware. Mankind's consciousness is awakening slowly but surely. Thy Will be done on earth as it is in Heaven. It is a promise from the Father.

The planet is cleansing itself and mankind is also, the traumas, the angers, and the fears are all coming out. As the people release, so does the planet, a total cleansing process. We are with you always.

Dear One,

I wish to tell you that humanities' values must change in order for an understanding of the Love of the Father for His children. The earth changes will bring about a comradeship, a fellowship of drawing the people closer together.

The need for humanity to assist one another will be greater, therefore forming strong bonds of love and caring. Natural disasters have a tendency to bond people and this will be so. Those that come to experience a transition at this time will do so. There is no loss of consciousness.

Pray for mankind, dear One. Your prayers and your petitions are honored and answered. Peace be to you.

Beloved Daughter,

I, Mary, wish to tell you that sharing is what the Father does, for that is Creation. The Father shares His gifts with you. The gift of love, the gift of speech, and the gift of being a co-creator with God in teaching, learning and healing. The Creator has shared His gifts with you, and you in turn share with your fellow-man.

You have been concerned about boasting. Dear One, boasting is of the ego, and you know full well when you fall into that attitude. An energy leak, as St. Germain calls it.

The merging of energies, yet never losing your own Identity with yourself and your Oneness with God and all creation is a wonder, is it not? There will be a deeper understanding of this for you.

Child,

Divine Love is a gift from our Creator, God the Father. The Love that encompasses mankind is the Pure Essence of God in Creation, although mankind is not totally aware of its' Oneness with the Father Creator. The day will come when all will know of their Divinity, this shall come to pass. There will be peace on Earth for a thousand years. It is a promise from the Father. Be in peace this day, Daughter of the Light. I am with you.

ஒ ⁂ ஒ

Dear Child,

The information we wish to impart to you concerns the ability to manifest anything your heart desires in the Light of I Am That I Am. One need but focus your intention with purity of thought and love, and manifestation becomes. It is the intent and the purpose that will hold the focus. Remember to focus your intent of allowing the Father to work through you in whatever manner He may choose. Do not forget who does the healing.

ஒ ⁂ ஒ

Beloved Daughter of the Light,

The wisdom of God is ever prevailing. There is no barrier in its application if one is willing to tap into the Infinite Source of all Knowledge. The essence of Who and What You Are is of God. That is all. Your essence is pure Light manifested into a body. All power is yours, because you are God. Thoughts that are not of your ego are the thoughts of the Creator, pure Love and Divinity.

In channeling from your God Source, the unknown becomes the known, and that is why we say all power is yours. All love is yours also, because you are the Love of God.

Beloved Child of the Universe,

Today this discourse will be on the Will of God. As the Creator cast you out with a breath from Its Thought, in that holy instant you were Its Will, part of Its wholeness, the Oneness of Who and What It is and Who and What You Are, Divinity expressing Itself! " And the Word was made Flesh". It is the joy of Love expressing Love. You are the joy of God and God draws you back to your rightful home. This planet is not your home. It is a third dimensional experience that you desired to experience for the fulfillment of your soul.

You are the Divine Will of the Father/Mother God in total perfection, fashioned after the image and likeness of Love, Light, Wisdom and Power.

Saint Germain

Beloved Daughter of the Light,

The great Divinity of the Father Source is What You Are. Your Oneness with the Father is set in stone so to speak, it is a Truth, and it cannot be denied in Spirit because the spark of Divinity is encased in your soul. That is Who and What You Are. The Father Creator is in you and you are in Him.

Divine Child of the Universe, your remembrance of your creation by our Father God is a gift to be cherished, and to assist you in your knowledge that there never was a separation. Be in peace this day always with our Father.

Beloved Being of Light,

Your Divine Light permeates throughout your beingness and extends out to Creation itself. Divinity is Who and What You Are. You are a manifestation of the great Creative Source, God. Love, flowing in all direction with the intake of breath and expulsion of breath.

The I Am is the Oneness of all creation, for We Are One. Humanity needs the constant assurance and the comfort that we can give them. Never fear, dear One, we are but a thought away. Just think of us and we are with you.

Beloved Being of Light,

Universal Love, the love of the Father is ever expanding and creating, for that is what Love must do. Creation is always in the flow of creating. You must become aware of your creations.

Any physical condition that is not conducive to the development of your soul comes from fear, no matter what form the fear takes. Fear is the great emotion of all manifestations that are not of Love.

Remember, there are but two emotions, Love and Fear. One comes from the Father Source and the other emotion comes from your ego. Do not give your ego this power. Negate all power from the ego.

Beloved Child,

We called you forth this day for union with us in service to mankind. Whenever more than one is in agreement for the good of mankind there is great healing for those who can accept and receive healing.

The heart and mind must be open, but as you know, the power of decision lies within each soul to reach towards the Light. However, petitions are prayers that are never lost, even though they may not be accepted.

We ask Jan, that the focus for this day be for the whole of mankind, and all of consciousness upon this planet. Be at peace.

Beloved One,

Oneness of mind, heart, and soul with the Creator Source is constant expansion in creation. When healing is being performed, the unity of two minds is activated and the force of God is drawn upon for the healing, whether it is for the physical, mental or emotional bodies. All is energy in thought forms. Through the power of love, healing, whether counseling, teaching, hands on, is from God, none other. Never forget that Child.

Daughter of the Light,

God's Will for you is you. You are the Will of God made manifest in a body, the Light of the Source. Nothing you say or do on this third dimension is of any consequence, for it is all an illusion. Only Truth is true.

When one opens the heart and mind, all knowledge can be remembered if one so desires. The blueprint of life is encoded upon your soul, and the remembrance of your abilities as a co-creator with the Father can be activated.

L'Morya

Beloved Child,

The information we wish to impart to you concerns the ability to manifest anything your heart desires in the Light of I Am That I Am. One need but focus your intention with purity of thought and love, and manifestation becomes. It is the intent and the purpose that will hold the focus. Remember to focus your intent of allowing the Father to work through you in whatever manner you so choose. Do not forget who is in charge.

Dear One,

It seems sometimes as though the transmutation of thought forms is forever tedious. However be aware that all thought forms are in the mental body. When you come from the point of love, then these thoughts are from your God Source, Universal Mind. Lifetimes upon lifetimes of thoughts that were not shall we say, in and for your highest good and do reside in you're mental and etheric bodies must be cleansed. It is why the Violet Ray mantras and rituals are so important, for cleansing and healing.

The Divinity of Who You Are, is always Pure.

Dear Child of the Light,

Stand in your power. All power in Heaven and earth is yours to be utilized for your own well being and for mankind. The strength and the power come from God, dear One and the right use of this becomes great wisdom. Wisdom is from knowledge, and knowledge is from the Soul.

The consistency of teaching, the consistency of chakra breathing, and the devotion and commitment to you, Child, is an expression of the God Source with you.

Beloved Child,

We will give a discourse on Universal Law of the Divine Will of the Father, Divinity in all its forms. Universal Law has an order, a balance, and a Oneness. It is Universal, coming and going, breathing in and breathing out. If you can picture the Breath of Life as an in and out, in constant rhythm, the pulse of Creation by the Creator Source. It is Universal, Divine, and all Oneness in the Totality of Love.

Unity, Oneness is ever present. With the breathing in and breathing out, creation is always being created by God, Universal Mind. *God is! There is and was never a beginning or an ending of All That Is.* That is why it is important to stay in the present moment, for that is all you have. Each moment is *Eternity*!

ତ ⁂ ୧

Child of the Light,

Your Divinity of God, for you are God in expression experiencing all that is to experience, is joy to the Creator Source, the Father. You are a beloved aspect of All Creation Itself, made to be a co-creator with First Cause and so that is what you are experiencing, co-creation. As you walk, hold the hands of your beloved Sananda the Christ, for truly He leads the way, for is He not the Way, the Truth and the Light? Blessed Christed Child of God, go in peace this day. We love you and are with you at an instant thought.

I, L'Morya support you and love you. Go in peace, Child.

ତ ⁂ ୧

Child,

We speak to you continuously, oh Daughter of the Light. The forces of God are always with you, assisting, guiding and leading you on your path of self-realization and enlightenment. Rejoice; rejoice, for there is great gladness in the hearts of those beings that are reaching for God, for it is in the reaching that one finds their Godhead. The constant longing of the heart for God the Creator Source is natural for the soul. You come from the Creator, so to be drawn back into Infinity is but the completion.

Quan Yin
Mother of Compassion & Mercy

Pick up your pen dear One,

Mastery over the emotional body takes time, dear One. When you weep as you call us forth, you are remembering the love, for did I not tell you that the heart remembers? Is this not what you teach in your Course in Miracles? That love in any form is love? No limitations on it, and we speak not of love of the emotions, but Love, Universal Love from the Mind of God. That is the Love that sustains you, holds your very cells together in your body. That is the forever Love of the Father.

Write this down, dear Child,

The dawn of each day brings hope to mankind because of prayer and petitions to our Creator for assistance. Know that all prayers and petitions are honored and answered, for the Father acknowledges all. Sometimes it may seem as though prayers are not being answered in your time as you know time, but know that time has no meaning to our Creator, and not one prayer and petition goes unanswered. The Divine Father knows every desire of your heart and honors you greatly, because you are He made manifest through Him.

Beloved Child, remember to keep your life simple, knowing that all is in Divine order. Know and feel that you are the Will of our Creator. The wisdom of God is ever prevailing. There is no barrier in its application, if one is willing to tap into the Infinite Source of All Knowledge.

Beloved Child,

The essence of Who and What You Are is of God. That is all. Your essence is pure Light manifested into a body. All power is yours, because you are God. Thoughts that are not of your ego are the thoughts of your Creator, pure Love and Divinity.

When channeling from your God Source, the unknown becomes known, and that is why we say all power is yours. All love is yours also, because you are the Love of God.

Dear Child of the Light,

The love of God is in the silence and also in this wondrous energy that is all around you. When one prays and meditates, a myriad of angelic beings come to attend and bring forth their energies to form a vortex of pure love. When two or more are gathered in the name of Christ, it is very powerful.

Great rays of lights stream forth to cover the designated areas for which you pray. There is cleansing, and healing on all levels of consciousness. Not only for physical beings but also for the planet, for as humans go through their traumas the earth does also.

༄ ✳ ༄

Dear One,

When one's life is in turmoil and confusion due to the circumstance of a dear one's imminent transition, the thoughts are not always centered, neither are the feelings, and the emotions can become disjointed, spreading here and there. Even the ability to pray and meditate can become a chore rather that a joyous event at these times. (Referring to the impending transition of my son Sal, who died December 14, 1998). Know that the Creator, our Father knows and understand this. There is no judgement and the Holy Christ Self carries you through these times.

The Saints and Angels, Jesus, Mary, the Masters all assist you for healing you and your loved ones, as you are experiencing this happening. You are never alone and we endeavor to infuse you with our energies of strength, peace in the heart and calmness in the knowing that "All is well, for God does truly care for all His Children, for are we not One?"

Be in peace, Daughter of the Light.

Beloved Daughter of the Light,

Holiness is your essence, for how could it be otherwise? Our Creator extends only Love, for God is Love and whatever extends from God is Holy, for You are the Thought of God, Divinity Itself. We are One.

Your perceptions are made with your senses of seeing, hearing, touching, smelling and tasting. These perceptions are made by the ego, which thinks its reality is real. In truth there is one Reality, your home with God.

This is an illusion that mankind is playing out, for it's desire to experience. It seems to be real. It is not. Peace be with you this day.

Sananda
Master Teacher of the World

❧ ✳ ☙

Daughter of the Light,

The consciousness of the world is rapidly changing. The Energy of the Christ is permeating the earth plane and also the cosmos. All of creation is being changed by this powerful Love energy. Planets, stars, universes all over, for are we not One? Our Creator is drawing His people closer to Its Energy. Go in peace.

❧ ✳ ☙

Pick up your pen Child,

When the Father created us we were created as pure Light, an extension of Himself and He endowed us with incredible powers. It is the misuse of these powers, the misuse of the Light, that has caused so much chaos and misqualifed creations. However, we also have the power to transform these misqualifications through our thoughts in the use of the Violet Flame.

The gift of free Will enables mankind to choose whatever path he/she will take in their lives. As you know, dear One, time does not exist and the option is always yours as to how you wish to live in this grand illusion. In any case, there is only One reality and that is Pure Light, Pure spirit and Pure Love. There is nothing else.

Once you are in tune with the Oneness of Who You Are, God, all of this will become knowledge. You will feel the Oneness, and doubt will vanish, for you will *know*. Take heart, dear One. We are One and we are always with you.

Pick up your pen Child,

Unity, Oneness of God is the only reality. We come from the Body of God. We are a cell, a Thought that is Divine, and all One. Unity burst Itself forth from its Universal Mind, a portion of All That Is, from the concept and energy of Love. Love, contemplating Itself to form Love, us, as sparks of Divine Light.

Oneness in Its' totality is complete, however, we are incomplete (mankind), until we are reunited with the Creator of the Universe, God. We are a tiny spark of the Whole. God in a sense, although complete, is incomplete until we are reunited with Him.

You see, dear One, in Unity there is no separation. There never was a separation, that is an idea made by mankind. How could there be a separation when you are part of the Creator? Your soul, dear One, is beginning to understand and feel this. I can feel that you feel our connection. You are taking us down from the pedestal, are you not?

You see Child, We are One.

Dear One,

Integrity is a powerful word indicating one's own commitment to one's self. One's spiritual attainment is constant if one is on the Path. The idea of reaching for the Father is ever present, for one begins to know that the reaching is the quest. The attainment is ever evolving, higher and higher. One never stays static, even when you think you are at a spiritual standstill. Sometimes, that is when you achieve some of your greatest growth.

Does not the stillness fill your heart with joy and bliss? Listen, for I speak to you. I want to assist you and I want you to know that we love you. Never forget Child, of the Father's Love that holds the focus of all. Stand in your honor and integrity as a Beloved Child of God.

Dear Child of the Universe,
Divine Being of Light,

Know ye that as time goes by the essence of your Divinity will become more evident to you. The intensity of Love that prevails in you for yourself, your Creator of all creations, will become clearer to you.

Mankind has little knowledge of their Divinity, their birthright and their inheritance from their Creator. Most of mankind is caught in a web of limitations, self induced and brought about by controlling factions of the religious that perverted the True Message of the Bringer of the Good News, Jesus the Christ.

Dear One,

His message of love and forgiveness (or release), was not understood because the ego was concerned about the third dimension. They, (mankind) did not understand about the spiritual forces. It was difficult for the people in my time, however, they tried and so it was a beginning for them on their paths.

Beloved Being of Light, the decision is always yours as to how far you desire to go on your spiritual growth. Know ye that the path is sometimes rugged, however the reward is great.

Remember that you are not your body, but a great beam of Light, a Thought in the Mind of God. Go ye in peace, Daughter of the Light.

❦ ✳ ❦

Beloved Daughter of the Light,

Know ye that all stems from the heart. All knowledge flows from the Akashic records, but first thy heart and mind must be opened. You must allow thy heart and mind to open so you may become aware. If one is blocked the awareness cannot enter.

The precious gift of free Will is Divine and corresponds with accepting responsibility and being responsible for oneself. Every human being on this earth, dear One, has what was given to me when I was Jesus. Awaken, awaken.

❦ ✳ ❦

Dear One,

There is some grief, a grieving of what will occur upon this planet, because you sense and feel it.

We will always be together in thought love and light, beloved Child. Did I not say that we are bound together from many incarnations? Dear One, we are energy, therefore how could we be separate?

Beloved One, it is good that you weep, for are they not tears of releasing? Know that I am with you always, and that I love you.

Dear One,

Meditation, spending time (for there is no time), in the focus of your spiritual growth is how the knowledge of Oneness is achieved! The more the heart opens to receive the Glory of God, the more it expresses the Love of the Creator, to God, to itself, and to mankind, for we are One.

When you know that the Source of Creation, God, loves you, all is possible. The yearning and longing slowly dissipates, for you know you are Love, and stand in the power and light of that knowledge.

Daughter of the Light, go in peace. We are One.

Dear One,

Everyone does not know the guiltlessness of mankind, because the ego is the symbol of the presumed separation from our Creator Source. Guilt was made by man to keep the idea of the separation alive, however the separation never happened.

Guilt is a tool the ego would use to keep you in the not knowing of Who and What You Are, a Holy Thought, a Divine Thought in the Mind of God. You are a Thought in the Mind of All Creation. The Father lives in you and you live in the Father. We are Oneness.

You (mankind), made the idea of separation and have sustained the idea of guilt that stems from fear, which stems from the idea that you could usurp the power of God!

I ask you, why would you want to keep such an idea that you and the Creator are apart? Is this not insane? See the insanity in the ego and choose once again, dear One.

Dear One,

Try to flow with all your feelings, your tears, your confusion, and the thoughts that are disturbing you. This is a cleansing and a releasing, so do not judge yourself. Accept it as part of your initiation. Great healing is occurring, although you are not aware. Stand firm in the Christed Being that You Are. Know that love, power and strength are there, but now it is just a mist in front of you.

Peace, be to you. You are learning and I am with you always.

Dear Heart,

The concept of mind, Universal Mind, God and Universal Light, being One and the Same is not easy to understand, however, bear in mind that the *understanding comes from your God Source that is One with God.* Your ego is incapable of understanding this because it is the part of your mind that is not of God, all understanding and knowledge are of God, our Creator. That is why the ignorance and the forgetfulness of his children sadden the Father, for they know not Who They Are. You are Love, and Light, co-creators in Unity with the Oneness of all creation.

Dear One,

When you weep you are releasing. Bless your tears, for are they not of God? The releasing and letting go is a process, a grand opportunity for healing. All must be healed for this is what the third dimension is about, a releasing and a healing on all levels, of the emotional, mental, and physical bodies. We understand and we are with you.

When you are in your holy place in your mind, the thought processes of your mind are thoughts of God. Even your tears are the tears of the Creator, for is not all of God?

Divinity is One, Allness in Love, purpose, design and order. Oneness of the heart, mind and soul, for we are One. The Light that you are, the desire of the Principle of God is Infinite.

Trials in your life are but third dimensional desires of the soul to experience and to remember, for all knowledge is yours, dear One.

Great Being of Light,

Oneness in Unity of the Creator Source, the Divine Will of God is your inheritance. You are a cell in the Body of God, that is the essence of God. The Creator wishes for you what It wishes for Itself, a total Beingness of Now! Experiencing Now, in this moment and in your brothers and sisters is all there is in the Love of Who and What You Are. This then affords you great freedom, to be free in your Divinity in heaven, as on earth. Go in peace, dear One.

ঌ ✳ ৰ

Dear Daughter of the Light,

You are as God created you, a portion of All That Is, a pure Divine Thought. Learn to think as your Creator thinks, for this is called creation. First, there is the thought, then the feeling, the desire, then the action. The Father Thought of you, therefore you are always in His Mind.

I am always with you, for thoughts leave not their Source. Go in peace and love this day.

ঌ ✳ ৰ

Beloved Being of Light,

Your Divine Light permeates throughout your beingness and extends out to Creation itself. Divinity is Who and What You Are. You are a manifestation of the great Creative Source, God. Love, flowing in all direction with the intake of breath and expulsion of breath.

The I Am is the Oneness of all creation, for We Are One. Humanity needs the constant assurance and the comfort that we can give them. Never fear, dear One, we are but a thought away. Just think of us and we are with you.

Beloved Being of Light,

Universal Love, the love of the Father is ever expanding and creating, for that is what Love must do. Creation is always in the flow of creating. You must become aware of your creations.

Any physical condition that is not conducive to the development of your soul comes from fear, no matter what form the fear takes. Fear is the great emotion of all manifestations that are not of Love.

Remember, there are but two emotions, Love and Fear. One comes from the Father Source and the other emotion comes from your ego. Do not give your ego this power. Negate all power from the ego.

ஒ ✳ ༄

Great Being of Light,

The consciousness of mankind will someday return to the One. It is so decreed and willed by the Creator, our Father/Mother. Those who cannot (or will not), return to the One Source will go elsewhere, for consciousness is never lost.

ஒ ✳ ༄

Daughter of the Light,

This beautiful planet is being changed and readied for a vibration of a higher dimension. All is in joyful anticipation for this dimensional change. The planet too is tired. She has been abused long enough. Go in peace, Daughter.

⁂

Daughter,

We are with you this day at Horton Creek. Know, dear One, that the Oneness of Creation is a gift of God, for we are part of the Creator God, with an individuality of personality. There is no one quite like you. You are unique in your individualization. In the Oneness, the At-One-Ment, we are all equal, for were we not made in the image and likeness of God?

The stones upon which you sit are held together by the force of God. This mighty creek and each drop of water, has God within it, a mighty power. The gentle breeze blowing upon your face is God, dear One. The trees, small shrubs and bushes all hold the essence of the vibration of God. The sun that warms your body is the Light of God, and the mosaic pattern in the water's movement is all God's vibration. The sunlight that also dances upon the water as the water moves in the streams and rivers is all tones, resonance, and beautiful colors.

(continued)

(continued from page 67)

Consciousness is forever changing, for in Creation the movement is. As you expand in Love, the resonance of your consciousness becomes finer and purer and also resonates at a higher vibration. You will understand this.

Loud noises disturb your consciousness, causing cracks if you will, in your emotional body, that is why you need a great deal of silence, so as not to upset your balance. Continue to put the Christ Light around you for protection.

We are One.

Beloved Being of Light,

Consciousness of God is ever in expansion, in the process of creation, for Love must extend itself. Love must share, for that is all It desires, and in co-creation with the Creator Source, this is what you do. The Love is the force that must be acknowledged as the only force of Creation. Creation does not exist without Love. The power that is yours is the Father's power, for you are endowed with everything that God has in the Unity of Love. Creation is constantly in the process of extending and as you are a part of God, so you extend in the Oneness of Who and What You Are, beloved child of God.

❦ ✻ ❦

Beloved Daughter,

That was quite an experience for you yesterday (I spoke at the, I Am America Conference, in Arizona), was it not? We are pleased. You brought hope to the beings there. This is how consciousness is raised, by the action of Love, the force from our Creator, our Father. Perfect loves cast out fear and the gentleness in which you spoke touched many hearts, dear One. Was it not a wondrous experience for you also?

We are One.

❦ ✻ ❦

Beloved Daughter,

Sitting in the quiet of your home in thought and meditation focused on God with the intent of the heart, dear One, is prayer. The commitment of your dedication to pray at night will be beneficial to you and pleases the Father. Anytime the focus of your prayers are for the good of all mankind, that is God within you praying, for are we not all God's children?

❧ ✳ ❧

Beloved Daughter of the Light,

Your unity with All That Is, is Oneness. A deep feeling and knowing of this wonder enables you to undertake any assignment that has been given to you, for on a level, you understand that is not you undertaking these tasks, but your Higher Self which always knows what It is about, and doing.

Tasks and assignments that seem monumental are but a second in your time and are accomplished effortless, for in truth your willing body does them, however with the Grace of God.

You are able to accomplish much when in co-creatorship with our Creator God! Go in peace, dear Heart in the Love of you.

❧ ✳ ❧

IAM That IAM

꧁ ✳ ꧂

Beloved Child,

Know that the Father always answers the desires of the heart if sincere and only He knows your heart. Place all your concerns into His care and ask for assistance and guidance. Pray for knowledge of His will for you and it will be given! The Father does not deny His children.

꧁ ✳ ꧂

Child,

The Oneness that you are is the true concept of Who and What You Are; a Divine Thought in the Mind of God. Energies are merged together to form a Oneship. Everything is in the Mind of God and is held together by the power and force of Love.

Consciousness is held in focus by the Divine inspirations of God. The Divinity of mankind is not totally known because of the belief in the idea of separation (ego-based), from God. The Temple of God is in you where God resides. Each cell of your body is a knowledge of God and vibrates that knowledge through sounds and colors.

৩ ✳ ৫

My Beloved,

By rights you are Love. Love never has to be earned. It Just Is. God created you in Love so therefore your Divinity is His Divinity. That is what you are, a Divine child of the Creator.

৩ ✳ ৫

Beloved Child of My Light,

The Divinity of mankind must be realized by every human being upon this earth. What good does it do oneself if no knowledge of your Godself is attained in a lifetime?

The discipline of daily meditations opens powerful forces in you. God forces become activated and the Christ force becomes more prevalent in you. Meditating daily builds a bridge and assists one in becoming more aware of its Christedness. Starting the day with meditation, and ending the day with the thought of God is very beneficial to one's soul. Sustain this simple ritual. Know you are Divine. Peace be to you, dear One.

❧ ✳ ☙

Child of My Heart,

Mankind has forgotten the intent and purpose as to why he came to earth, to experience the senses without forgetting his true Identity, as a holy child of God.

The mastery of the emotional body is an attribute of a Master. Practice non-judgement daily. It is a great accomplishment. Learn to bring all misqualified thoughts into the Violet Ray for transmutation. These misqualified thoughts (energies), have adverse repercussions not only to you but also to mankind and the ethers. Judging one's brothers and sisters restricts your knowing. Remember that judgement and harshness of thought, comes from the ego. As you are a child of God you have the power to change your consciousness through the power of Love. Go in Peace, Daughter of the Light.

❧ ✳ ☙

Dear Daughter of the Light,

Oneness is knowing that you are a Divine Thought in the Mind of God, its essence being Love. Attaining the knowledge of Oneness is the awareness that we, the children of God, are All One. There is nothing else. Divine Thought, Creator of all Creations Thought of you and so it is. The essence of the Divine Will of God is you, for you are the Thought in His Mind and that is His Will. What God Wills Is, and is held in focus by Love.

The consciousness of mankind is being raised and eventually all will know their holiness. There will be Peace on Earth.

All is expanding and forever growing, always to higher levels, so that the Creator may experience all.

❧ ✳ ☙

Beloved Child,

In silence the Creator is found. Feel and experience the Love that is around you, it is as though just for an instant, everything has stopped breathing, for love is so great in the vibration about you! When God burst Himself into Its Creation, It was through Its Love of Itself.

❧ ✳ ☙

Beloved Daughter of the Light,

The Will of the Father is you, for you are the Will of the Father. When the Creator burst Itself into its creations it was through It's Love of Itself.

The desire of the heart to know thyself is a portion of All That Is returning to It's Source, for it must return to It's Source for It's wholeness. One becomes whole in Christ to the Father. One's Christ is the link to the Father. The Creator is *never separated from Its Creations.* Ask yourself, are you separate from your creations, your love of your family, your music, and your love of plants?

❧ ✳ ☙

Child of the Universe,

The Universe is Oneness. The Universal Mind is All That Is, the Alpha and Omega, the beginning, the end, but there is neither beginning nor end. Evolution (God), goes round and round always meeting Itself. The awesome power of Love is the Force of the Creator.

You are a brilliant light.

❧ ✳ ☙

Beloved Daughter of My Heart,

The Creator is constantly pulsing in Its own Divinity, ever evolving, expanding and growing in consciousness. The Universal Mind must create for as It creates, It is extending Itself, Love creating Love.

All of mankind one day will experience the Oneness of the essence of Who and What They Are, for We are One. Go in love and peace this day.

❧ ✳ ☙

Daughter of Love,

The Universal Mind of the Father is Love in constant Thought, always being and ever evolving in Universal Love, for Its essence Is.

❧ ✳ ☙

Child of the Light,

Petitions and prayers are heard. Know that as you think in terms of Divine Love, those are the thoughts of the Father. When a thought of Love in any form comes from your mind, it is coming from the point of Love and the point of Love is *always from your Father, Who is Divine Love.*

༻ ✳ ༺

Beloved Child,

Great are the Thoughts of Divinity in all It's Glory, in all Its' vibrations of sounds and colors. Keep the thought of God ever in your heart. Live your life in and for the Love of the Father, then everything you do is a prayer. Go in peace.

༻ ✳ ༺

Beloved Daughter of the Light,

The Universal Mind of God is pure Love, Love in all of its forms. The creative Forces of the Great Source are the strength, power and the wisdom of All That Is. The Beingness of you, the Light of you is what you are. Light, lowering its density to take on the body. Once you make a commitment to come to this planet Earth, you must experience all, and so as you experience all, so does the Father, for is not the Father within you?

Beloved child of the Father's Mind, concentrate on accepting your Light body, with and in conjunction with the idea that you are the Light in your Father's Eye, forever shining, and shining. Go in peace and in the Love of God.

Beloved Child of God,

Everyone does not know the Divinity of mankind. Each soul upon this planet is God, made manifest in His Image and Likeness, created by Love, to love. Souls are sustained by love only. Mankind is not always aware because the ego (idea of separation from the Father), has become dominate and mankind has forgotten Who and What He is, pure Love, pure Light and pure Divinity. We are the Beings of Light who surround you. Go in peace, Daughter.

❧ ✳ ☙

Child,

The Presence of God, the Creator of all creation is always with you. How could it be otherwise, Your Holy Christ Self, the Divinity of Who and What You Are is also with you, and is there for you to access. Call upon your Christ Self for wisdom and answers. It is yours Child. Be not separate from your Christed Self, for you and the Father are One.

To become totally Christed, one must negate all ego thoughts that would interfere with your well being. Retain Child, only thoughts that are coming from the point of Love and that dear One, is coming from your Christedness in all things.

The intent and desire of your soul is to be fulfilled in this lifetime. This is what you came to do. It is your completion, dear One.

❧ ✳ ☙

Beloved Daughter of the Universe,

Your meditations and devotions to God the Creator of All, sustain the purity of the heart and mind. It is the intent and the desire of your soul that is manifested, though you may not always be aware on this plane of existence. The love that you carry in your soul is the love of the Father, for is not All That Is, Love? It cannot be otherwise for Creation (God), is forever expressing Itself for its fulfillment of its desires.

Beloved Child of the Universe,

We wish to impart (for We Are One), the concept of wellness in the body with the power of thought. It would be well to guard your thoughts, for manifesting is occurring rapidly, and as you know it is in the mental body that *all* and we repeat *all* illnesses of the body occur first.

What you judge will always be returned to you for your learning and understanding, because you will draw that experience to you, dear One.

ᘐ ✳ ᘏ

Daughter of the Light,

The Unity of Oneness and Love of the Creator, in the spontaneity of Creation within Creation, in the Oneness of All That Is, is your Divine inheritance, your rightful inheritance from the Creator. Know the grandeur of the Thought of Who and What You Are, a Thought of the Divinity of all Life. There is no separation it is an impossibility! You need but choose to remember your Divine essence of the Flower that burst Itself in continuous bloom, ever unfolding, ever blooming.

Love the Source of it All.

ᘐ ✳ ᘏ

Beloved Being of Light,

The Oneness of All Creation is in Its' ever enfolding act of Creation and is forever evolving. As you evolve, so does the Father, as you experience, so does the Source of all Creation. As the Source is in you and you are in Oneness with God, Creation explodes in expansion. So be it.

Beloved Daughter of the Light,

Power, love and wisdom are the gifts of knowing Who and What You Are. The Christ of Who You Are is What You Are. The Christ essence, the Holy Spirit never forgets the Father of all creation, it is the link to the Source. Think child, of the times you have assisted mankind; no matter the motives of your ego, it was and is the Christ within you that is and does the work of the Father. Never forget that, dear One. Goodness only comes from Our Creator, none else! Only God may call Himself/Herself Good.

Beloved Child of the Universe,

Beingness is constant. The Will of the Creator is ever in movement, a pulsing, a breathing in and a breathing out in the totality of Love creating Itself, knowing no boundaries, and no limitations, only Being. The wind that gently blows is being, the birds that fly are in their beingness. The stillness in the plants is in its beingness. The gems and stones are also in their beingness. In silence can the Voice of Universal Mind be heard, Knowledge Itself remembers.

Beloved Being of Light,

This discourse will be on the Unity and Oneness of All Creation, of the Thought that brought you forth and Oneness in the Idea of All That Is, Creator God. You are a portion of God, the Source of Power, Love and Light that resides within your Being.

Honor, honor yourself, for as you do so, you honor God, the Great Spirit within you. There is no greater love than the love of you, loving your Creator, and as your love of God increases, the love of you increases, for We are One, We are Unity. And so it is, I Am.

Beloved Child of the Universe,

The love essence of the Father is constant creation. You are an aspect of the Universal Mind. *Love must extend itself, therefore you are Love's extension, and as you are Love's extension, you must also extend.* Your creations are an extension of God, which is Love in a constant thought of creating within Creation.

Dear One,

If you but pause to look at the reflection of your soul (the Light of you), and the morning sunlight, you will see they are one and the same. Light, dear One is what you are, not your flesh body, but your Light body. It is your Light body, the thought behind your Light body that creates. That thought is sustained and held by the focus. It is your thought that manipulates the Light. The sustaining of Thought holds all Universes by great Beings of Light.

Dear Daughter of My Heart,

Have you not heard that silence is golden? The love that you have for the snow upon the ground is a reminder of the feeling of Oneness with the Creator. Snow symbolizes the purity of All Creation, in it's stillness and flowingness. Each beautiful flake is the magic and essence of God in all His Glory. Dear One, snow is soothing to your heart and mind. The beautiful serenity of All That Is, is in each snowflake and that is what you sense and feel in your Beingness.

ᔕ ❋ ᔓ

Beloved Daughter,

The surrounding of all life to Life itself, is the Creative Source. Eternal Love is ever present, it is the force behind those tears, for must not the Creator also feel through you? Tears, dear One, are a releasing and cleansing for the soul.

ᔕ ❋ ᔓ

Pick up your pen, Child,

Feeling guilty is a grand ploy of the ego, to keep one from focusing on their Divinity and Holiness. Keeping one in that state of emotion and mind dampens and prevents truly knowing and experiencing Who and What You Are. Your choices are made in your thoughts, and thoughts are powerful, they do create and create they will.

You, dear One, make *anything detrimental to your well being, so guard your thoughts. Remember and live your Holiness in your Christed Self in your connection with the Creator of All.*

Daughter of the Light,

Go slowly, dear One. The assimilation of your recent journey takes time. You will absorb all that occurred in Calgary. Go slow, dear One. Be not impatient with yourself, go with the flow, and weep your tears, for weeping assists in releasing misqualified energy.

Dear One,

The Spirit of God within you is your sustenance, and being in constant Unity with the Father is a given. The energy of the Creator Source is ever evolving, therefore so are you. Each moment of evolution is eternity in action in its grand display of now. In practicing living in *now*, you are experiencing *simultaneously with God in all His Glory!*

Expansion of consciousness is constantly in movement, flowing and ebbing like the ripples of water, flowing out and flowing in. The Father delights in your Being, for are you not His Creation by His Divine Thought? Go in peace this day.

Divine Being of Light,

Guiltlessness is the order of being Divine, for it is a natural state of Being.

Realize you are a Cosmic being (the Light of the Creator expressing Itself), in whatever manner the soul desires to express and experience, so it will know itself in the completeness of the Love of Who and What It Is.

The word guilt is a word without meaning unless you so choose *to give it meaning and power and control over you. That is your choice however (guilt), is foreign to our Creator, God.*

The wind blows and the trees sway in the wind, does the wind feel guilty because the trees sway and do the birds that build their nests in the tree feel guilty? All are expressions of consciousness of the Creator. Humanity too, is expressing, extending and creating, all in and for the Glory of God, forever and forever.

Dear One,

The energies are affecting you greatly, however, you can use these powerful energies (those that are not in the Light feel more disturbed), and turn this to your advantage in practicing more *love, balance and more compassion for yourself and mankind.* It is all choice, dear One. Stay in your determination to utilize these energies for your spiritual growth.

Beloved Being of Light,

Oneness in the Creative Source of God is All That Is. You are in the Mind of God, a Thought that does not leave It's Source, for All That Is, is forever creating and expanding. As you expand, the Mother/Father God expands, for creation is always in movement, a pulsing, a breathing in and a breathing out, like the tide. Time stands still for there is no time. Creation just is. It is always happening now, the *Eternal now*, no past and no future, only *now in the Oneness of Creation.*

Daughter of the Light,

Oneness in Unity with the Great Central Sun, our Creator God, the Source of all Love, and all Light is constant. It just is. One may deny and not accept this knowledge and truth, however it (denial) does not make Truth an untruth. Truth is Truth, even though one's perception of Truth may be at a different level, still the Truth of Who and What You Are is constant, it never changes. You are a pure Being of Light of the Body of God, a Thought of Love, by Love for Love.

❧ ✳ ❧

Greetings Jan,

What a joy to be with you on this second day of the New Year. Your dedication to the Creator of All Creation is commendable. We applaud. Know that We are always with you with but a thought, for is not all thought, dear One.

❧ ✳ ❧

Beloved Daughter of the Light,

Know ye thy thoughts of Love are the Thoughts of Thy Father. Thy heart is filled with Love for mankind, and Thou prayers are heard. Walk in peace this day, Daughter of the Light.

ஒ ✳ ௸

Beloved Child,

All illusions are but that, illusions, in any form, for they are but dreams. Dreams merely mean you are asleep and Truth has not been brought to the illusion. Either you are awake or not. In dreams are illusions acted out without the thought of the Truth. In reality the *Truth is All There Is*, then the playing out of the illusion dis played with joy and love, for the knowledge has not been forgotten. Daughter of the Light, the knowledge is there, it but needs remembering. Lift the veils, oh Daughter of the Light, for herein lies your joy in *Truth.*

ஒ ✳ ௸

ஒ ⁂ ௐ

Beloved Child of God,

Oneness Is, for the Creator of all Creation is Love in energy form, therefore you are energy, a portion of the energy of the Body of God, a cell in the Body of Love Itself. Love is ever expanding in perfect synchronization, in balance and harmony.

ஒ ⁂ ௐ

࿐ ✳ ࿐

Beloved Child,

Thou are blessed. We watch over you and guide you in all your endeavors. Stay fast on your holy path in love, devotion and in a steadfast manner.

࿐ ✳ ࿐

☙ ✳ ❧

Beloved Daughter of the Light,

The Light of Who and What You Are, the Light Essence of the Creator is your Oneness with all of Creation. God desired and so It Was, so It Is, and so It Will ever be, forever and forever.

In great joy is the silence of your soul, experiencing the Oneness of Thy Creator. Peace be to you, Beloved of the Light.

☙ ✳ ❧

❦ ✳ ❦

Beloved Being of Light,

The Majesty of God our Creator desires to express all things in consciousness.

❦ ✳ ❦

Dear One,

Unity with the Divine Will of the Father is constant. It is but your desire, for the Creator breathes that desire into your soul. It is energy that must acknowledge itself for itself. It is Love acknowledging Love and Love expressing Oneness, It is, I Am, I Am. Beloved Daughter go in Peace.

Daughter of the Light,

Your journey will be one of great significance (referring to my trip East for the birth of a grandchild). The love that you bring to that family will be healing for them and for you. Remember that each new soul that takes the flesh is a wondrous event and you will assist that soul as well as the other souls. Let that be our focus on this trip of love and compassion. We love and support you in your endeavor.

Dear One,

Salvation is of God. As the thought of separation occurred to mankind, the Creator provided an answer, the Holy Spirit. As we are in the Body of God, the Father knew the idea of separation was not, however, we needed a means to return to Him, for we are comprised of this Love, and Love returns to Love. *The Holy Spirit* (your Higher Self), is the means by which we awaken to *Who and What We Are.*

Divine Being of Light,

Oneness is the Body of God, Universal Mind, One Body, and one Cell in the Body of God. God Thought, and so It Was, It Is. Extension of God Source is what you are. Mankind limits the Creator, in it's concept of God, for God is energy ever expanding in consciousness.

Divine Child of God,

The Oneness of the Father in you (for all is One), is in you and mankind, and all universes. The Oneness is the Universal Mind of God in all things. The Love energy is all there is of All That Is, the constant Source of Creation. You are an extension of that Creator, a co-creator in the principle of Love. Creating your heart's desire is the Father's heart desire, for you are an expression of God made manifest upon this third dimension.

Beloved One,

Creation in the birth of a new baby, a new soul, is surely “more of God to love”. Beings of Light are being born throughout this planet for the feminine energy to come through for the “Peace on Earth” as promised by our Father the Creator.

Go in peace and love on your journey, dear One.

Beloved Being of Light,

Oneness in all its form is Oneness. When ye tap into the All That Is which is you, God within you, the Universe within you, (all universes), that Oneness is you. All That Is, is you, God force within you with all knowledge, power and strength. Love is Who and What You Are. You are the grandeur of Divinity forever and forever. What you Are is What all of Mankind is, there are no separations, only perceived separations. Your Divinity can never be altered for how can you alter what your Creator created? All is Divine, All Is.

Beloved Being of Light,

We as One in joint Universal Mind, ever expanding and ever creating continuously in the state of Beingness, are Divine Love in action. First there must be the thought, the desire (feeling) and then the action. God contemplating Who and What It Was, and Is, then the desire of the Isness, and then the bursting forth of Light, Life Force.

Judgement, dear One, does bind you and keeps you in bondage. The soul desires to be free, and the cells in your body desire to be free also, for is that not God? Freedom is an aspect of God of all Creation.

ঌ ❊ ঌ

Beloved Child of the Light,

Forgiveness is an aspect of the Will of the Universal Mind, although the Creator Source, the Father of all Creation knows that there is nothing to forgive, for all is an expression of God. Mankind needs to experience and forgive itself in love and compassion. Each soul must release its pain. The learning is presented now, for Now is All There Is.

ঌ ❊ ঌ

~ ❋ ~

Dear One,

The world offers exactly what amount of energy you would allocate to it. It is true you have your needs on a third dimensional level, however, if one knows in their heart's mind, the lack of importance of this worldly dream (for it is a dream, of which mankind has not awakened), the dream can be altered and changed. The *awakened soul, mind and heart experiences with the Mind of God, and is aware of this illusion and gives it but a passing glance as it chooses to stay awakened.*

Beloved Being of Light, the Oneness of All Creation rides on the rays of Light.

~ ❋ ~

৩ ☀ ৬

Child of the Light,

Creation belonging and being in the Father is experiencing the now of Eternity. *Eternity is forever happening. The Father is experiencing as you experience, for you are an expression of Divine Thought. So Be It!*

৩ ☀ ৬

Daughter of God,

Salvation can be said to be the purpose of your life on this planet for your going back to the Creator Source and the understanding of the idea of Who and What You Are. It is also the gift of the Holy Spirit, your Higher Self, which is the connecting link between you and God.

This Holy Week focus on the message Christ came to bring, by His willingness to be an example for us, in His Resurrection, proving our Divinity in Spirit.

ᘏ ❊ ᘓ

Dear One,

Consciousness has been raised at a level that you will soon understand. Already you are experiencing the effects of the energies. We are always with you, dear One. Mother Mary knows your heart love and what you experienced with your sister. Dear One, realize there is a purpose in everything and you will accomplish what you desire to do. A disruption is not really a disruption. God the Divine Presence uses all.

Go in peace, dear Daughter.

ᘏ ❊ ᘓ

❧ ❋ ❧

Beloved Being of Light,

The Divinity of Who You Are never changes, whatever you feel. Feelings are an aspect of the humanness, however, it does not take away from your Holiness.

Those who doubt, doubt with their humanness, the ego. Doubt can be brought to the Holy Spirit for a change in perception.

We are always with you. We are but a thought away.

❧ ❋ ❧

ঌ ⁂ ൡ

Beloved Child,

The answers are within you, dear One. Be patient with yourself. All is in Divine Order. You are cleansing; it is a releasing of energies and old ideas that no longer hold truth in them for you. Letting go of thoughts takes time, as you know, it is a process. In a way this is an initiation for you.

ঌ ⁂ ൡ

Beloved Daughter of the Light,

Eternity, the foreverness of God is never diminished for expansion is forever. God knows only Creation in Thought, for all is Divine Thought in action. You are the effect of first Cause, the Creator.

Align thy thoughts with the thoughts of God, for His Thoughts are Holy, and holiness is your Divine inheritance, for that is what you are, a Divine Child. Beloved Being of Light, we are One and Oneness in it's universality in the great Mind of God. Co-creation with God in alignment with the Divine Will of Creation is Godliness in Action.

Child of the Light,

Oneness in its creation is forever creating. When you are in completion, you go to the oversoul. The oversoul waits for all it's parts to return to it, then the oversoul with its collected parts returns to the Oneness of God, the Creative Source of All, for God Is.

The Love of God for mankind is never measured for we are the only Creations of God in total Love. God cannot be otherwise for Love is the Force of All Existence, the Force that holds the universes together.

Dear One,

The consciousness of mankind is changing. Prayers are the greatest force of assisting in changing the consciousness to a greater love of itself, which is God. Every prayer, every thought form, from your Holy Christed Self, and (all thought forms of Love are from the God that You Are), is God in expansion, sharing and experiencing uniquely through you. Because each cell is the body of God, God desires to experience through you every experience that is possible.

Beloved Being of Light,

Oneness with and of God, Solen Aum Solen Is. The Love of the Holy of Holies, the Cause of all Creation, cannot be comprehended with one's mind. It must be from the heart.

Consciousness of God is Oneness for all is God, All That Is, and The Holy of Holies. The Consciousness of God is expressing itself through you. You are God in form and your true form is Spirit in the Oneness with the Creator, who is all Love, all Encompassing, all Divinity and all Holiness.

Know thyself, know thyself! Love thyself, for thou cannot do otherwise, for Love, loves.

Daughter of the Light,

Know that thou Divinity in unity with the Creative Source in that total love is Universal law in action, not only in this dimension but all dimensions of consciousness. The Father's desires are your desires, for are you not One? The experience of experiencing life is just that, an event in your consciousness, an illusion on this third dimensional level.

As you co-create with God, the love expansion goes out in waves of consciousness in tones and colors, and as the majestic resonance of God expands so does all of mankind, love extending, love expanding in pulses of energies.

Beloved being of Light, Daughter of Divinity,

Our Oneness in Oneness with the Father is perfect Love with all of Creation, for there is none other than God's Love which is the Source of all Creation.

The trees that bow down in total adoration of God and the trees that stand tall reaching to their Creator are in silence just being *in consciousness, loving and expressing its Oneness with and in creation.*

Daughter of the Light,

Daily prayers for you and for mankind are most pleasing to the Creator. That is how one co-creates in unity with God. The love that is in those prayers goes forth in pulses in waves of consciousness, like ripples upon the waters that the oceans feel throughout, from one side of the ocean to the other side.

❧ ✻ ☙

Beloved Daughter of the Light,

The Universes are mine, sayeth the Lord God of All Creation. Not one hair upon thy head is unnoticed! *All is from God.* The blade of grass, the pebble of sand and the water, each drop containing the essences of the Lord Thy God. The stillness, the wind, all unseen and seen is of the Lord Thy God! Beloved Daughter of the Light, I accept your love, for are we not love? Love creates dear One.

❧ ✻ ☙

Dear One,

Consciousness of God, the Isness of All Creation, is Creation Itself. Beloved, when you became a Thought in the Mind of God, It Was. Thought is so powerful. It is thought, desire and action that create manifestation. God is always creating; ever expanding and so are you. You are creating with the Universality of God. That is your purpose, your consciousness is expanding and evolving so the Father can experience through you, for are you not God?

Amen and Amen, the Father and I are One.

Daughter of the Light,

The joyousness of Life! The celebration of being alive in your spirit of your God Self is indeed wondrous! Perfection, being Itself, for it cannot be otherwise. All is Light and the Light of Who and What You Are is but a portion of the Creator Source. You are endowed with the power of God to co-create with Him, and indeed your creations are blessed, for you are the Divine Will of the Father. Remember to align your Will with the Divinity of God's Will, for it is God's desire and yours also, as you are One with All Creation.

Dear One,

Oneness in consciousness. We will give a dissertation upon this. The consciousness of God, total Love in desire of the thought of you, and you, and you, your brothers and sisters of Creation, is ever expanding and pulsating, for God creates and His Creations are perfect in total Holiness and Oneness. Your creations when viewed with and created with the Mind of God are also perfection, for are you not God in desire and action?

Walk in holiness, in truth, justice and gentleness with love and compassion.

Daughter of the Light,

Being in and of the Light of God is really all there is. As you experience all feelings upon this earth you are learning about the emotional body and you are learning that this is part of the third dimensional aspect of life upon this planet. Feelings are to be experienced, felt, looked at then released without judgement.

❧ ✳ ❧

Daughter of the Light,

I, Thy Lord God wish to tell you that mankind will know Itself, will know that I Am the Creative Source and Force that created them out of My Love for My Creations. Mankind will come to know that My Gifts of Life Force are to be used in a loving manner. No more will my children put upon another the burdens that are theirs for their own enlightenment. No more will My children dash the children in utter lack of honor. No more will the brothers and sisters (my creations), inflict harm upon one another!

I Am Thy Lord, Thy God and so I speak.

❧ ✳ ❧

Beloved Daughter of My Light,

Oneness in Creation; all is God. The implosion of God in His desire to create was indeed a marvelous event. *God Always Was and Always Is.* How wonderful that our Creator extended Itself, for we are the result and only Creation of Our Source. Our own creations are in Oneness with Our Father, as above, so below. As the Father extends we too must extend, for are we not an extension of our Creator?

❦ ✳ ❦

Child of the Light,

The concept of the abstract essence of God and one's ability to love an abstract essence is difficult to understand. Your Beingness rests in God, and is God by its own right.

❦ ✳ ❦

❧ ✳ ☙

Beloved Daughter,

You are One with and in all creation; One with the universes, the planets, the stars, moon and the sun. One with the masters and teachers (our brothers and sisters), and one with mankind. One with the waters that flow upon the earth, the beasts that roam, and the plant life that supplies oxygen, we are One with Universal God, Our Mother/Father. There is no separation, for all energy (God), comes from God. *The Idea of Us Was and Is in the Mind of the Creator and So It Is.*

Creation extends itself for it must create in Love, for that is the purpose. Love extends and shares; therefore we as mankind extend and co-create with the Father Thy Source.

See thyself and see God. See thy neighbor and see God, for there is no separation. Love extends love in all of Creation.

Thy Child of the Light, go in peace this day.

❧ ✳ ☙

❧ ✳ ❧

Beloved Daughter of the Light,

God the Father created you in image of Itself, and endowed you with all of His energy of co-creation.

❧ ✳ ❧

❦ ✳ ❧

Child of the Light,

Perhaps Oneness is difficult for mankind to understand. Dear One, you come from the essence of the Creator, our Father. Father Thought of us, and So It Was. Oneness with all creation, the universes, the planets, the skies, the ethers, below and above, for there is neither above nor below, there is only That Is, God. The Eternal Presence is all there is, for that is creation in expression, always Being.

The mind cannot understand this concept, precisely because it is the mind, but this is understood at the intuitive and heart level. It is a knowing, and this knowing requires but a remembering. All information is gathered in your soul, and thou knowest this. The veil is heavy and a willingness to let go of the heaviness will bring back remembering. All information from the Creator, Source of All, is given to you. The Father must share, for sharing is love in action, and you, as a species must share also, for you are co-creators with Universal Mind, God.

The love of our Creator for His creations, you, cannot be explained or defined, for there are no words to express, for all is vibration and color.

Peace to you, Daughter of the Light.

❦ ✳ ❧

Divine Child of Universal Light,

Beingness is constantly in the process of being. The Creator, the Father of All is forever expressing and expanding. The great expansion of the universes is exploding at all times. The spark of Love is always in expression. There is always and always. Creation never stops and it never started, *It Always Was, and Is.*

Dear One,

You are and ever were a Thought in the Divine Mind. Love must extend and create, for Love goes into Itself and implodes Itself into Creation.

Remembering is opening the mind and heart to allow all new thought to enter into, without the ego interfering and causing blocks to be put up against all Wisdom and Knowledge of the Father. What you think you think from the mind, however, allow the flowing of God thoughts to replace the ego thoughts. The ego will always rationalize and place into a set pattern the ideas of itself, whereas the thoughts of God are a knowing in your heart and mind. You don't even have to think. The thoughts are just there, and you have a confidence and a wonder, as to where did this come from. You know that these thought did not come from you.

Beloved Child of the Light,

Do not underestimate the power of the ego. The power that you assign to it is how you make your creations. If you come from the point of Love, from God, there will never be pain or disappointment!

Learning how to discern when assisting another can assist you in becoming aware of controlling entities. Be aware of these entities that misuse and use their ego self as a means of getting their way. Send them love and light and do not get involved with them and go on with your life.

There are people who are constantly in the ego, and know this, they do not want to know any other way! The word manipulation is not only a word, this is how many people live, never wanting to accept their lot in life, so they cast their wills upon their brothers and sisters. Remember that one can only plant a seed in the mind of another.

Dear One,

Unity in God and in all creation, in mankind, the plant kingdom, the animal kingdom, the planets, the suns, and all of the twelve universes is a Truth. The Creator, the Father and I are One, you have heard many times, in times past and also in the book that is called the Bible.

When there is pain in humanity, all consciousness feels the effects of it. The misqualified energy of mankind is also felt by the earth, and so the earth is traumatized as well as mankind. That is why it is important for mankind to pray for mankind, sending love and light wherever it is needed. The power of many people unified in thought, focusing on assisting in healing mankind and the planet is very powerful. It is the intent of the soul and the desire of the heart and mind to heal that is beneficial, and the Brotherhood of Light assist you, for it is all energy focused in love and power of God for the purpose of healing.

❧ ✳ ☙

Beloved Child of the Light,

The Universal Light of God forever and forever shines. It shines upon its creations, in total delight and bliss. *It is in At-one-ment with Itself and It's creations and is eternal in the Beingness of Itself in the Eternal Silence.* God is joy in the celestial music of Its Beingness.

The God that you are is an aspect of this Divinity of Itself. God Is, God Was, God Eternal and Eternal. **B**eloved Child, do not forget your Divinity, honor it, bask in the glory of it all. What a Creator God, to give us an aspect of Itself.

Go in peace and love this day.

❧ ✳ ☙

Beloved Child of the Light,

This is Holy Easter week, the fulfillment of what My Son came to do upon the earth, for you see dear One, his mission was to enlighten mankind and to show that there is no death, yes, a death of the body, but not death of an Eternal Being. You are of my essence, Pure Thought, Pure spirit, where death cannot touch. *We are One, We are One*, and I would not allow my precious creations to be harmed, for indeed you were created to co-create with *Me, I Am, I Am.*

Precious Loves of My Light, My Children, surround yourselves with the glorious radiance of the Holy Christ Golden Light. Enjoy this Easter Week in the knowingness and bliss of All That Is, in peace, love, and compassion for yourselves and your brothers and sisters.

Daughter of My Light,

In God we live, in God we love and in God All Is. The purpose of mankind's enlightenment is just that, to become enlightened in you're daily life. One need not perform vast and great things. It is the daily consistent effort of living each day in love and in *peace* with great *compassion* and total *forgiveness* of self.

When you consider that the Creator, our God allows everything, that is what allowing means. To live one's life as best as one can and to be aware that if the Father does not judge anyone (including you), then one does not have the right to judge anyone, including yourself.

If you are aware that God in His Divine Wisdom is totally aware of every event that is occurring in your life, then is He not aware of what is happening with everyone else? Are not your brothers and sisters as important to our Creator as you are? Become aware that judgement of any kind is misqualified energy causing you pain, and also the person whom you judge. Be at peace and surround the entity that you judge in the White Light of God.

❧ ✳ ❧

Beloved Child of the Light,

This Holy Week is celebrated throughout the world. It is the Resurrection, the New Life, the Awakening. There is no death, there is no death! Alleluia, Alleluia!

❧ ✳ ❧

Daughter of My Light,

Oneness of heart, mind, soul and body in unity with all of creation in union with the Creator Source, Universal Mind is all there is. It is the Beingness of Being that gives joy. The act of just living in the now is expressing the love of Who and What You Are. One needs to do nothing! The essence of God within you, about you, yea all around you is expressing, for God never stands still, so to speak. God is forever expanding and unfolding in Its Love for Its creations, and dear Child, so are you! Go in peace and love this day in unity with All That Is.

ஓ ✳ ல

Daughter of the Light,

I Am in You and You are in Me forever, forever and forever. Eternity (and that is what You are), is in a constant motion of Being. The moment of now is all there is in All That Is, in expression and expansion of Creation, in the expression of Love. *The many forms of love, dear One, are expressions of the Father manifesting in you.*

ஓ ✳ ல

Beloved child of the Light,

We enter into a new communion of the perception of Love and Light of I Am That I Am. The Glory of God, the essence of Creation Itself, for it is all God, all power and might, all encompassing and never ending! The Angels are continuously singing the praises of the Glory of God. The spherical music of the harps is played in harmonious rhythm in the Glory of Creation Itself. The myriad of God's Creations is all in total rapture with and of the Love of God! The heavens and the stars, the planets and universes dance in joy and brilliance, in and for the Glory of God, thou Creator. Go in Peace and Love in total communion with thy Creator this day.

❦ ✻ ❦

My Child of the Light,

Time as you know time is collapsing into a no time. Consciousness is becoming more expanded. As you expand and grow in consciousness, and become more enlightened in the knowledge and the remembering of your God Source, your Divine thoughts are going out into the Universe and the consciousness of mankind is being affected.

The Oneness, the Love and Light of Mother/Father God is being extended. All mankind, when thinking loving thoughts and living their Godliness upon this earth is assisting in changing the energy of consciousness. As above, so below, dear One.

The Creator Source, our God, does not desire anything that does not bring happiness to Its creations, and you, dear One, are the creation of God. Remember, if what you do does not bring joy, peace, and a deep feeling of contentment in the heart, ask yourself if you are coming from the point of Love. Always remember, any disturbance of your Beingness, is being caused and created by you. If the feeling is uncomfortable, that is a clear signal for you to present this experience to the Holy Spirit, the Christ Self, for a shift in perception. The *Christ always answers*. Develop an attitude of patience and deep knowingness that you *will get the answer, at the time (for there is no time), that you will be able to accept*. For the answer is already there, for to the Holy Spirit a problem is a problem and no different whether big or small.

Beloved Child,

When one's emotions seem to be in utter turmoil, know that this is an opportunity for great spiritual growth. Allow your emotions to flow, take a moment to experience what you are feeling, ask yourself if these emotions are for your well being. Remember that all is from God and all is allowed by the Creator Source. Make no judgement upon your emotions, rather, bless them, for this is part of being human, and choose to learn from these feelings you are expressing or experiencing. Remember that the ego will always delight in keeping you in guilt and confusion. This dear One, is not of God. The Creator wants only peace, joy and a deep contentment for you. The Love of the Creator will and does heal all perceived situations. The Holy Spirit is ever waiting for your decision to bring every problem to His attention so healing may occur.

Beloved Child of the Light,

More and more of mankind are expanding in the knowledge of their true inheritance, knowing their Godhead. The Creator has given us all attributes of our true Beingness. When mankind awakens and realizes that whatever we do, if done in the name of God is a prayer, there is healing. This is how we change consciousness. Every holy thought that extends into the Universe is like a ripple of water. Likewise, every unholy thought has the same effect. We are co-creators with God and co-create we must.

Beloved Child,

Joy in the heart is an attitude that can be developed by the mind when one chooses to look at and experience life from the point of Love. Choosing to live in the world, yet not being of the world can be mastered if indeed practiced daily.

How easy life seems and indeed does flow when one lives in the attitude of graciousness and gratitude, gentleness and Divine Love. Living the attitude of love and acceptance can ease all of the misperceptions in the manner in which you view and live your life. So be it.

Daughter of the Light,

The joy of creation is brought about by love. Your creations that are created by love are an aspect of God. Man is a co-creator with God, endowed with all Its' gifts of the ability to create. Child, the essence of the Creator within you is the force behind your creations. God's love for Its' creations is an extension of Itself, passed on to mankind. Mankind too must extend the love of God, for that is its desire. Man was made to love and extend that love in sharing. That is the desire of the essence of Who and What You Are! It is the reason for your existence.

Beloved Child of the Light,

The Love of our Creator for Its creations (us), is so vast that the human mind cannot grasp the total concept of this glorious reality. It is the only reality, for in Truth you are not your body, but a great beautiful light of the Universe. The essence of your reality is pure spirit, pure energy, created by the desire of God. The Love of God Is All There Is and That Love Is What You Are. You are not separate from your Creator, but an extension of God's Mind. Give thanks daily to the Cause of your existence.

Child of the Light,

Eternal is what you are, as an extension of the Creator. God is forever, therefore so are you. Your body is a vehicle for God's energy to manifest itself. The love of Who and What You are is all there is. Honor and nourish this physical body for it is the Temple of God.

The love that is within you cannot be contained, for it must create, because you were made to co-create. When you create your creations with love, you are coming from your holy God Force. However, when you make your creations you are coming from your ego. There is a difference between what you have made and what you have created. Truth can only be in one, and the power to decide whether you desire to create or make is yours, because free will is God's gift to you. Recognize that one's creations (from love), will bring peace, balance, harmony, and great joy in the heart and soul, whereas what you make from the ego is temporary and not nourishment to your soul.

Child of the Universe,

In living your life, each day bless everything that you say and do, indeed consider everything blessed. For as you are a holy child of God, a holy manifestation, everything you say and do is blessed. Keep that thought in mind. Allow your creations to be created with the Thought of God.

Our Creator sees you in total perfection, for everything that comes forth from Itself is perfect. Striving to develop the habit and daily discipline of practicing loving yourself as the Father loves you, will eventually become the only way you will want to live. Stay in communion with your Creator in all situations, conditions and events in your lives. Practice calling upon your Holy Christ Self (the link between you and God), in all situations. The answer is always given; however, one must be willing to hear your Higher Self.

Be sure that if your answer does not give you peace and joy of the heart, you have not heard the correct answer, you have listened to your ego. Remember that in asking the Holy Spirit for help you must be willing to accept the answer with trust and faith that God knows what you need.

Beloved Child of My Heart,

Learning how to simplify and enjoy one's life is truly an art and form in itself. When you awaken in the morning, start with a greeting to your Creator and with an attitude of gratitude because you have awakened. Ask for guidance and direction in fulfilling your obligations for the day. Learn to keep the focus on each moment, for indeed there is only now. This takes much practice, for the human mind seems to enjoy the dreaming of projections. When you consider that all you have is right this moment, life seems and indeed becomes easier and simpler. The effort itself is effortless. For as each moment is lived in its entirety and with full concentration on itself the tasks become lighter and lighter. Projection tires the mind and emotional body. It is unnatural to the human condition. Your Creator created you to live in full freedom and that not only means freedom from outside persecutions, but inner ones made by yourselves. For it is your thought forms that prevent and set up blocks to your Divinity as a Holy Child of God. Freedom is a holy aspect of God to be experienced by His children in all things and at all times.

Beloved One,

When you plan your duties for the day, and often it is over planed, and at the end of the day your chores are not finished, some of you choose to feel guilty for not completing those tasks. If the Father created you and I assure you that He did, that Source that created you is in you, about you and around you. Now, consider that if you allow yourselves to feel guilty then you are judging God. Remember that the *Temple of God is within you. In judging yourself you are judging God and if you allow yourselves to feel guilt (an aspect of the ego), this is your choice.*

God allows everything upon this free will planet. It is impossible for God's creations (mankind), to sin. Mankind's miscreations have been brought about through the ego and its ignorance. The message that Jesus came to teach was for each person to forgive, for he knew that these brothers and sisters that were killing him were coming from their egos, and their fears.

Beloved Child of the Light,

Love is the healing energy of the Creator Source. Love heals all things, all persons, situations and events. This Love of the Father is powerful and is for your use. Because you were created from the pure Love and Desire of God, this gift of love can be used to heal. Instead of choosing to come from the ego mind, which will always come first, you have the ability to change your mind and activate that force of Love to heal any situation, condition, person or thing, because you are a *Thought in the Holy Mind of God.* This Love is not an idle energy; it is a pulsing vibration of the finest and highest frequency and is in constant involvement in the evolvement of mankind becoming.

When you activate this love, which is your love, you heal at some level of consciousness, not only the person, situation, or place, but also yourself at the same time. Healing is never alone, it always involves other consciousness, because we are One in God and affect every thing that lives. From the tiniest grain of sand upon the shore, to the vastness of eternity, this Source is Love.

Beloved,

The Christ that You Are, the true You, can manifest healing through the Power of God. It is not the Will of God for mankind to be ill. Illness was man made through thought forms of miss-creation. As a small incision upon your finger first heals from the inside and extends outward so does your spiritual growth. It is an inside job. Healing on any level can be accomplished with an acceptance that this is an act of Divine Love. You were given free will and that choice belongs to you. Healing the spiritual, mental, emotional and or physical bodies takes but a willingness to accept the Love of our Creator as the *Primary Source of Healing*. Choose well, oh Child of the Light.

Daughter of the Light,

Each individual that becomes aware of God within is slowly changing the consciousness of mankind. This changing of the consciousness is a collective effort. Just one person coming in unity with its Christed Self affects many others. As we are all One in God, every event that occurs upon this planet affects all human beings and indeed all consciousness. Great acts of love (the ultimate sacrifice of Jesus), impacted all of creation. Even so, acts of violence go into the consciousness also.

Beloved, spending time in prayer and meditation for your biological family and for the welfare and well being of all humanity, is how the minds and hearts of mankind is awakened. Mankind needs to pray for one another, because we are all part of one another in the Sonship of God.

There are no accidents. There is a purpose in all that takes place upon this planet. *When there is a tragedy of great significance all of mankind in one way or another are affected and great changes for the good of humanity often follows.*

❧ ✻ ☙

Beloved Daughter of the Light,

Know that as the great energies of Love and Light are being poured upon this planet earth, every human being is being affected. Indeed all of consciousness is being changed, the animal kingdom, the plant kingdom and the mineral kingdom. As the earth prepares itself for the massive changes that will occur upon its body so does mankind. Every cell in your molecular structure is being affected.

Accept more and more *light* into your body structure, for you are *light*, which lowered itself to take on the body. As the Light of the Creator is becoming more prevalent upon this planet, the cells of the body are changing. It is wise to flow with and to honor the many changes that you feel are occurring within you.

The physical body feels different to you, and the mind and heart also, for you perceive your life in a different manner. Situations that bothered and upset you are no longer upsetting you, and you are wondering why. Your desire and need to be silent and for solitude is increasing. Pay attention and honor this need, for it is in the silence that the Father speaks to you. Begin to know Who and What You Are.

continued

You prepare yourself for the massive earth changes by knowing your Divinity. Realize that you will experience what the soul came to experience, and if you are told to move from your physical location, then do so. You may also be guided to stay where you are, then indeed, honor that. You are being gently led upon your path so you may fulfill your soul's desires. No one will be lost, for all is energy coming from the Creator, and can the Creator our God lose Itself? The Thought, that you are from the Creator's Universal Mind, can never be misplaced. Go in peace and love this day.

Beloved Child of My Light,

When each child of Mine discovers and remembers that I Am One with you and all mankind, division amongst my people will cease. As I created you in Love, your one driving force is Love. The only Source of all healing is Love. This is My gift to you, and it is not to be abused in my Name. There are no such things as holy wars! *Would I, the Creator of all Creations ask any of my beloved people to kill, mutilate and commit atrocities upon each other. Think upon this, you who would kill one another in the name of justice and in My Name. Wake up My beloved people!*

Daughter of the Light,

One must be consistent in desiring to attain a higher level of God awareness in your life. A daily discipline of calling upon the Creator for assistance in all your endeavors in your life, can become a habit after a while. This will increase your awareness that you are not alone.

Beloved children of My Heart, if you only open your eyes to see, and open your ears to hear, you will see and hear the Masters whisper to you. You are constantly surrounded by your angelic guides to comfort and assist you. God does not abandon His Creations. Children of My Light, go in love and peace this day.

A Letter from the Publisher

Dear Reader:

It is within our mission to publish spiritual works that are gifted to humanity for the purpose of raising the vibration on the planet, and to assist in our awakening to the age of peace.

This book was published verbatim as it came through to the author from the Masters. We recognize that some of the grammar usage, and typestyles may not reflect what we might consider to be "proper". However, we were spiritually guided in the pubishing process to leave these words unchanged.

We acknowledge that letters, words and sounds each carry distinct vibrations. It is our personal assessment that the precise wording in these messages hold the vibrations of Divine Love, Divine Peace and Divine Compassion.

It is our desire, as publisher of this book, to insure that the contents convey the specific energy that the Masters and the author intended.

Peace and blessings to you.

Infinite Light Publishing

About the Author

Jan Manzi was born in Island Falls, Maine; a small town in Aroostook County, near the north-eastern border of Canada, in a family of three sisters.

Through her life's journey she has been guided to and has developed an ancient Egyptian form of healing.

Egyptian Healing is an ancient method of working with the electro-magnetic energies of the body, aligning and balancing the mental, emotional, spiritual and physical bodies of the client. Pharaoh Djoser was a healer in the Third Dynasty and oversees all of her healing sessions.

This healing work consists of implementing her tonal soul name, Ilaniuani, music, color, toning and channeling as guided.

Jan became a channel one day when she was sent to a stream in Arizona, by El Morya and he instructed her to bring a tape recorder, pad and pencil. There she received her first channeling by Mary. Then after prayers and meditation at home she would hear, "Get your pen dear One". Thus, "Reflections on My Eternal Light was born.

❧ ✳ ☙

In the Light of the Creator . . .

We See Only Love

❧ ✳ ☙

www.ingramcontent.com/pod-product-compliance
Lightning Source LLC
Chambersburg PA
CBHW032046090426
42744CB00004B/106
9780967872131